"This book of one-page insights begins with an introduction and prologue and then focuses on the themes of goals, seeking positive energy, development of the personality, God's reach, and relationships. These are followed by notes, which are a listing of six goals to individuate designed to help individuals realize their talents and callings. The overarching theme is about moving towards inner peace, joy, acceptance, love, and unity through psychological well-being, specifically through a connection with God. Each page gives ideas, then says to "keep it moving." This encouragement is followed by ways to move on. Such ideas include finding one's purpose through listening to one's soul and trusting God, having one's own positive narrative, following a God-given pathway, sitting in silence, listening to God, and utilizing healthy communication skills.

This small book of basic insights can be utilized easily by anyone needing a quick reminder of ways to meet goals in life, connect to one's inner self, and connect to others and to God. Each reading has a specific insight under a common theme and can be easily accessed by the heading. The ending notes personalize the book by having the reader summarize what they have learned from these meditations. The book truly can be used as a meditation as each reading can be read and explored through meditative practice. The author's work is written in a thoughtful manner and can easily be incorporated into one's daily practice. This practical guide may prove highly beneficial for those looking to draw closer to God."

**—The US Review of Books**

# KEEP IT MOVING

Meditations on Overcoming Obstacles and Living Your Best Life

## PAULA RAINER, PH.D

Archway Publishing books may be ordered through booksellers or by contacting:

Archway Publishing
1663 Liberty Drive
Bloomington, IN 47403
www.archwaypublishing.com
844-669-3957



One verse from the Common English Bible under
Favorite Quotes: "Don't judge, so that you won't be judged.
You'll receive the same judgment you give".
Matthew 7:1-2

ISBN: 978-1-6657-3543-8 (sc)
ISBN: 978-1-6657-3542-1 (hc)
ISBN: 978-1-6657-3559-9 (e)

Library of Congress Control Number: 2022923488

Print information available on the last page.

Archway Publishing rev. date: 03/29/2025

Do not waste another second, minute, or hour of
your life stopping at physical, emotional, or cognitive
barriers that undermine your purposeful life.

This book will provide you with tools to quickly recognize
barriers and how to keep it moving to walk over, around
or under these barriers so you can live your best life!

# DEDICATION

I dedicate this book to my heavenly parents, David, and Renee Bluford, who taught me the philosophy of keeping it moving. My husband, Stuart, is a calming force when I need to keep it moving. My three children, Chadwick, Camille, and Christina and grandson Chadwick Jr. have walked the journey of keeping it moving through successes and adversity. They are all inspirations to me beyond measure. Their love and strength propel me to keep it moving for my lifetime.

# *ACKNOWLEDGE*

I want to recognize Fr. Donald Heet for helping me to navigate my spiritual goals of balanced well-being. He has given me insight to continue to achieve God's journey for me to keep people moving forward to internal peace, love, and belonging. I want to acknowledge Dr. Thomas Monteiro, who is like a dad to me and a guiding force of love, acceptance, validation, peace, and a steady spirit. Marlene Alexander, my California mother, helped me grow as a woman and wife through my 20s to 30s. I appreciate my sisters Pamela and Penny, who make up the three "P"s; no matter what, we always come to conclusions of unity and Brittany who is an outstanding mother to my grandson.

# INTRODUCTION

These meditations include philosophy, wellness, and spirituality narratives. Use this book to walk in your truth and fulfill the instructions of your soul. The reflections are in chapters like the chapters of our life.

Clients, colleagues, and counseling students inspired this book by asking me to repeat words of philosophy and meditations I had just imparted to them. It would be hard to capture the same essence again when they asked me to repeat my comments. So, I started to record these words of wisdom on a notepad.

I accumulated multiple quotes and notepads, so I put the most memorable quotes in a book. We experience a range of emotions daily, whether mindful of them or not. We stream through positive, negative, and neutral energy experiences daily. Emotions and psychological well-being are indicators of how we navigate our experiences and relationships on the earth and how we cope with these encounters. Our DNA plays a part in how we manage these encounters.

Likewise, our environments and relationships generate positive, negative, and neutral emotional and cognitive responses. This book helps people to navigate their lives and achieve their hopes, dreams, and goals despite their past development or current state.

Free your mind and open yourself up to new possibilities. Walk through life mindful of valid frameworks which develop your purpose and soul. Positive energy, faith, balance, and peace represent your destined pathways. So, seek positive narratives and keep it moving.

# *PROLOGUE*

As a child, I was always open to the lived stories and insights of my parents, grandparents, aunts, uncles, and elders. I listened because I respected them, and I knew they loved me. I did not realize that one day their words of wisdom would benefit the challenges I would encounter. I needed to understand how these nuggets of information would build my resiliency based on their lived experiences.

It is better to build resiliency by understanding other people's experiences instead of suffering the same fate. Learning from your own lived experience without guidance from others can create a perspective of unnecessary pain and suffering.

Empathic listening and knowledge gained from the lived experience of others builds sustainability without being exposed to those experiences yourself. Your time on earth is limited based on years and the encounters with people you can experience. However, you can put a multiplier on the understanding of life if you gain knowledge from others.

Take advantage of learning from other people and build your durability from their experiences. It is better to learn from others who can impart lived experiences, adaptability gained, and brackets for problems in the future. Therefore, keep your mind open to the learned perspective of others.

The people who I learned from the most are my mother and father. My parents lived experiences developed resiliency garnered from their belief in their independence to thrive. They were self-made in many respects and did not entertain barriers for themselves or others. They did not let health, a lack of bestowed generational wealth or a guidebook for career success hold them behind a wall of hopelessness. Instead, they leaned into their own learned experiences, which developed resiliency and led to their individualized and collective success.

My mother and father (David and Renee Bluford) kept it moving and did not let anything external to their belief system or barriers stop them. They demonstrated faith on the path to their goals, and they were able to arrive at their destiny with room to help others.

The multifaceted generosity of their time, money, wisdom, guidance, optimism, strength, and abounding hope spilled to their daughters and the community in Queens, New York.

Their strength proves that if you have hope to transcend your challenging episodes in life, you will develop strong shoulders to overcome complex life events to help yourself and others to realize a fulfilled and fruitful life.

Keep it moving, learn through resiliency, and live your optimized life with a greater perspective of inner purpose which teaches us about hope and creating the life we desire.

# CONTENTS

**GOALS**


Chapter 1:    No one else can see your purpose ................................... 1

Chapter 2:    Perfection is an exercise in futility ........................... 2

Chapter 3:    Always love yourself through struggles ....................... 4

Chapter 4:    Allow doors to shut when they are closing .................. 5

Chapter 5:    Run quickly or softly toward your goals ..................... 6

Chapter 6:    Stay away from a dim star ....................................... 7

Chapter 7:    If you are sitting alone in a room with a
magnificent idea flowing through your
brain, and there is no hype or cheering
squad, do not worry.......................................... 8

Chapter 8:    Ask yourself if failure is a goal ................................. 9

Chapter 9:    Our destiny is individuated and authentic................... 10

Chapter 10:  We all feel that we have walked a trillion
steps and have at least a trillion more steps
in front of us ................................................ 11

Chapter 11:  Make yourself a profit center of survival on earth........ 12

Chapter 12:  Do not follow the goals and dreams of someone else ... 13

Chapter 13:  Life is a journey of many questions............................ 14

Chapter 14:  Distractions from your positive narratives
are destructive to personal development,
goal completion, and long-term mental health.............. 15

Chapter 15:  If you believe you are a procrastinator, it
has more to do with your belief system
about yourself than the acts of procrastination ............ 17

**SEEK POSITIVE ENERGY**

Chapter 16: We decide to walk through positive or negative portals of actions, behaviors, thoughts, and emotions ..... 21

Chapter 17: Negative energy is always chasing everyone everywhere, every day ..... 23

Chapter 18: Do not act on negative thoughts or deeds toward others ..... 24

Chapter 19: While on the journey of life, sit in joy ..... 25

Chapter 20: Some people exercise harmful parasitic activities to selfishly access their needs by taking advantage of people's talents, reputations, and overall good energy ..... 26

Chapter 21: It is good to be decent, kind, humble, and unselfish when there is nothing to gain and no one is watching ..... 28

Chapter 22: If you are in an environment where your talent thrives, do not assume that your emotional energy is also thriving. ..... 29

Chapter 23: Do not focus on judgmental people ..... 31

**DEVELOPMENT OF THE PERSONALITY**

Chapter 24: Many people fear being great ..... 35

Chapter 25: When you are talking to someone and want them to listen, you must be formulaic about starting a discussion ..... 36

Chapter 26: When you say that you care, it is not an automatic act of caring ..... 38

Chapter 27: Acknowledge negative thoughts and anger ..... 39

Chapter 28: Autonomy does not mean selfishness, self-absorption, or self-importance ..... 40

Chapter 29: It is essential to recognize when you are worrying nonstop ..... 41

Chapter 30:  When you know your worth, the road will
            open for you ............................................................... 43
Chapter 31:  Many people exhibit morality and hold up
            the mantle of righteousness for others to follow ........... 44
Chapter 32:  You can do internal work on yourself to
            deal with the external world ......................................... 45
Chapter 33:  Many people live a symbolic life that makes
            sense only to them from their selfish lens .................... 46
Chapter 34:  Do you feel invisible in the world, like
            walking around an altered existence be-
            cause your core personality is kind and gentle? ............ 47
Chapter 35:  It would be best if you never let age define you ............ 49
Chapter 36:  What does it look like to transfigure yourself? ............. 50
Chapter 37:  Instead of trying to follow someone else's
            blueprint, ignite your life narrative ............................. 51
Chapter 38:  It is important to note that popular pur-
            suits are already known and executed .......................... 52
Chapter 39:  A receptive vessel of humanity will always
            listen to your narrative ................................................ 53
Chapter 40:  An executive is not necessarily sitting in the
            executive chair ............................................................ 54
Chapter 41:  Parents already have a strong spiritual bond
            with their children, so they do not need to
            make a mirror version of themselves ............................ 55
Chapter 42:  Some people think that when they have
            been received, endorsed, or hired, they be-
            come great at that moment .......................................... 57
Chapter 43:  Some people fear expressing their emotions ................ 58
Chapter 44:  Where you are is not where you must be or stay .......... 59
Chapter 45:  People forget that they have an expiration date ........... 60
Chapter 46:  You already know the answer if you are
            questioning, feeling uncomfortable, or ask-
            ing for advice about an ambiguous situation ................ 61

Chapter 47:  If you love humanity, you will examine
           how often you sacrifice, stand up for, or
           help your fellow man ........................................ 62
Chapter 48:  Are you trying to make things friendly and
           pleasant when they are not? ........................... 63
Chapter 49:  A bully has an objective to diminish the
           person's sense of self ..................................... 65
Chapter 50:  Anxiety is a knock on the door that some-
           thing is bothering us ..................................... 66
Chapter 51:  Are you sensitive? ......................................... 67
Chapter 52:  When you value a house, chair, or sofa
           more than those who sit on the furniture
           or live in the house, your chairs and house
           will eventually be empty ............................... 69

## GOD'S REACH

Chapter 53:  God said to trust and meet Him at the highest point .. 73
Chapter 54:  We all have a road to Damascus moment
           where we are humbled ................................... 74
Chapter 55:  Get on the zip line with God and hold on ................... 75
Chapter 56:  Sometimes, people try to steal your peace,
           grace, and mercy ........................................... 76
Chapter 57:  A perfect storm is when God wants you
           to wade in the water to trust and walk
           through the murky water to get a blessing ................. 77
Chapter 58:  Do not let people weaponize your love of
           God against you ............................................. 78
Chapter 59:  Do you have constant contact with God ................... 80
Chapter 60:  On some days, 1 + 1 equals 0, and every-
           thing adds up to a negative value ................... 81
Chapter 61:  Hell is a mountain of judgment that you
           project and receive ........................................ 82
Chapter 62:  Forgiveness is freedom from the chains of
           what someone else has done to you ............... 83

Chapter 63:  Sometimes, we blame God for our chal-
lenges and say it is our cross to bear ............................. 85
Chapter 64:  The power differential constantly shifts in
organizations that promote a power base ..................... 86
Chapter 65:  After you have tried to talk to someone to
solve a problem without success, look internally ......... 87
Chapter 66:  Receiving God in your life means accepting
the humble gifts that He has put on your soul ............. 88
Chapter 67:  The walk with the Creator feels lonely at
times because your walk with the Creator is
unique and unmatched ................................................... 89
Chapter 68:  When you follow the pathway of God, your
plans are already fueled ................................................. 91
Chapter 69:  The world is a place to discover more of
God's goodness in people and unique places ................ 92
Chapter 70:  If you are no longer dreaming and inspired,
remember that fear and hopelessness are
probably present ............................................................ 93
Chapter 71:  If we love ourselves or others blindly with-
out first attaching to the humble Spirit of
God, we will not make room for greater love ............... 94

## RELATIONSHIPS

Chapter 72:  The number of positive relationships pro-
vides the ingredients for a positive life ......................... 97
Chapter 73:  Do you feel isolated, although social media
gives you access to millions of people and
opportunities? ............................................................... 98
Chapter 74:  Existing without good communication
represents existence without being seen or
heard authentically ...................................................... 100
Chapter 75:  What is your relationship with money? ..................... 102
Chapter 76:  What is your relationship with human frailty? .......... 103
Chapter 77:  Leaders serve at the pleasure of those they lead .......... 104
Chapter 78:  What is your relationship with anger? ...................... 105

Chapter 79: You might find yourself in a relationship
where you pull the most weight financially,
socially, or professionally ............................................. 106
Chapter 80: Your success or failure is impacted by other
people when their feelings or thoughts affect you ...... 108
Chapter 81: What is your relationship with the sunrise? ............... 109

# GOALS

# CHAPTER ONE

# NO ONE ELSE CAN SEE YOUR PURPOSE

Your purpose is on your soul at birth. There is an internal soul light that you can feel. It shines outward when you share your gifts with the world. Your dreams will become a reality when you put your purpose into action.

Refrain from expecting people to understand, endorse, support, or help you with your purpose. Your vision rests in your unconscious soul only. Successful people will understand your need to follow your inner soul. People who have not followed their inner souls will tell you why your goals are impossible.

Keep it Moving:

It might take your entire life to figure out how to fulfill your purpose and vision. But it does not matter how long it takes; get there, even if it is a fraction of your goal. It will still be a profound accomplishment.

The satisfaction of fulfilling your purpose will validate your struggles, pain, suffering, and negative energy. Your purpose is the unique blueprint that you must follow. Your mind, body, and spirit will navigate you to the instructions of your soul. Do not allow people or obstacles in the universe to place you on a predictable and marginal path that does not follow the instructions of your soul.

# CHAPTER TWO

# PERFECTION IS AN EXERCISE IN FUTILITY

Perfection is an infinite goal based on worldly normed standards that are forever transitory. Normed standards of perfection are constantly changing with the changes in society's fluctuating ideals, beauty, power, economics, intellect, and pop cultural shifts. These changes are too numerous and fleeting to follow as goals to perfect. These are goals of futility. Instead, focus on the achievement of goals that you create. You are more likely to achieve goals grounded in your control and motivation.

You can never see the top when you climb the mountain of perfection because the peak continues to grow with the changing standards of perfection in the world.

So, beware when climbing a mountain of perfection with no end. You will spend endless time climbing due to outside influences. Instead, it is best to climb a mountain of achievement that embodies your internal goals. The mountain of achievement is finite because it represents your set internal goals with coordinates, duration, and a measurable peak.

Keep it Moving:

When you stop following normed standards of perfection and start your internal goals of achievement, you will be successful and satisfied. You will climb your mountain of accomplishment, which makes you internally proud, not externally validated.

Perfection in isolation should never be a goal. Mastering your standards should be the goal, not externalized perfection. Following someone else's ideals of perfection makes you exhausted, resentful, and somewhat bewildered about what is next. Therefore, a mountain path of perfection will make you continue to look for external instructions.

However, on the mountain of achievement, you will embody your standards and goals to accomplish your dreams. The peak of achievement represents your end goal. It can be easy or difficult, but it is all within your hands. So always be aware if you are on the mountain of perfection or achievement.

So, follow your road, not the road of others. Find your mountain of achievement and accomplish your internal goals. Master your standards and live a life of dreams normed by you only.

# CHAPTER THREE

# ALWAYS LOVE YOURSELF THROUGH STRUGGLES

Include a vision of hope that will never fade. Love yourself first and foremost, regardless of unhappiness or distress. The love of self will allow you to soar through storms. Remember that you are strong and possess the skills to transcend any battle.

Love yourself enough to know that the battle means that you are alive. Within life, you have many choices to neutralize difficult times. Face your struggles head-on with your eyes wide open, and the light will shine on possibilities of change. Be patient. The light might not come immediately like a flood light, even if it is a flickering light, bask in the glimmer of light. If you choose to succumb to your struggles, the light will slowly dim and turn off. Your drive to live a fulfilled life will also slowly turn off.

Keep it Moving:

Carry a virtual flashlight in your hand and light your way to affirming solutions along the road of struggles. Do not be the one to turn off your light of strength and possibilities. Other people might try to dim your light but remember that you hold the light in your hand to transcend struggles through self-love.

# CHAPTER FOUR

# ALLOW DOORS TO SHUT WHEN THEY ARE CLOSING

Be brave and look for another open door, window, or peephole of opportunity. Or construct your doorway of opportunity. When we are too comfortable, we do not move to the next level, thing, or blessing because we are sitting behind a closed door of complacency. To move to a higher gift, God shuts the door, so we have no choice but to move forward. Sometimes we are shaken up and thrust down so we can crawl, stand up and walk toward God's protective arms.

Keep it Moving:

Blessings are not stagnated but move as our needs change. Therefore, staying in a passive mindset is not a goal. When things slow down or seem to stop, that signals that a door is closing or has already closed, and it is time for you to move forward.

Even if the change seems unexpected, trust that God has your back, and He knows when your current state will not lead to continued development. We are supposed to develop our authentic and individual achievement continually. Therefore, continue to look for and seek blessings of change to elevate and implement obedience to God's focus on your development.

# CHAPTER FIVE

# RUN QUICKLY OR SOFTLY TOWARD YOUR GOALS

The speed matters less than the mission to stay within your goals. Your dreams become a reality when your inner spirit is propelling you forward.

Keep it Moving:

Roadblocks, negative energy, and mishaps are put in place to distract you from your goals. It might be troubling that you cannot move some barriers, but they help you to understand every aspect of your destination. After your obstacles have educated you along the road of life, you will learn how to focus on your goals and harness positive energy to accomplish your dreams.

# CHAPTER SIX

# STAY AWAY FROM A DIM STAR

Dim stars are people who do not have your best interest, but they are managing, mentoring, or impacting your development. Refrain from engaging people with limitations in the areas you need to develop. Their limits will become yours. You will never move past their knowledge to successfully fulfill your vision.

Instead, seek a mentor who values your talent and can help you develop your full potential to transcend higher goals. Every failure you have encountered are unconscious limitations you have set for yourself, including the mentors you choose.

Keep it Moving:

Continue to know yourself and where you are going. Then, choose a mentor based on your internal calling and their willingness to see your contributions and innovation to the world. Mentors who promote your transcending development are willing to help you excel in the future. To choose the right mentor, you must know your worth, where you want to go, and a visualized pathway to your future.

# CHAPTER SEVEN

# IF YOU ARE SITTING ALONE IN A ROOM WITH A MAGNIFICENT IDEA FLOWING THROUGH YOUR BRAIN, AND THERE IS NO HYPE OR CHEERING SQUAD, DO NOT WORRY

You are not alone. You are standing in the abundance of your internalized soul energy.

Keep it Moving:

No one else needs to stand in the room beside you. It only takes one person to believe in a dream and one to take the first step to make it happen. Be brave and take the first steps to put your idea into reality. The vision is yours, and it is up to you to move it forward. Get started on your organic path without any other ingredients needed.

# CHAPTER EIGHT

# ASK YOURSELF IF FAILURE IS A GOAL

Are you pursuing aimless pursuits? Is failure an unconscious goal because nothing is moving forward or planned? Are you randomly bumping from one thing to the next? Are you busy figuring out who you are so you do not have to get started with your goals? This aimless work is not a movement toward a goal.

Do you have a history of looking at failure like it is a familiar friend? Do you have stories of childhood when you disappointed someone because you made a mistake or did not succeed at something? After this encounter, did you feel like failure was an identity rather than a single act? Have you continued to make failure an identity instead of an attempt to succeed? Did you create continued narratives of failure and anxiety around failure? If you did, your development around failure is flawed. If you subsequently devalued yourself due to mistakes, you are now responsible for removing these negative narratives.

Keep it Moving:

Trying, stumbling, and failing because of attempting goals is the ingredient of success. Likewise, the playbook of dreams coming true embraces failure as a necessary factor for achievement.

When you are focused on internal goals, you will not let micro failures stop you. However, focusing on external narratives and plans of others will make failure a life goal instead of a step toward success. Failure is a stride toward achievement, not an identity.

# CHAPTER NINE

# OUR DESTINY IS INDIVIDUATED AND AUTHENTIC

Do not consider opinions that stifle your authenticity. Authenticity is bending into your uniqueness and not being afraid to celebrate individuality. Most people learn to be free and accept their truth after they have lived a lifetime and time is not on their side. However, regardless of age, our destiny never leaves us. Our ability to continue to exist on the earth lets us know that we still can individuate and live authentically on earth.

Keep it Moving:

You can actualize your destiny daily at 10%, 50%, or 100%. Never give up. Fulfilling your individuality might mean seeking a different pathway to maturate an abundant life. Transition into your new path and create new goals, objectives, and mentors to help you realize a destiny of abundance and truth.

# CHAPTER TEN

# WE ALL FEEL THAT WE HAVE WALKED A TRILLION STEPS AND HAVE AT LEAST A TRILLION MORE STEPS IN FRONT OF US

We must be mindful of fulfilling the steps ahead by not perseverating on the steps of the past. Have you ever tried walking backward? Walking backward is not natural? So why do we look back and reflect on our past and try to relive it or correct it?

Focus on what you learned from the past that you can apply today. However, do not focus on the negative energy of the past. When we focus on history, we need a better sight line of our path ahead.

By focusing backward, you might trip or become disoriented. So, avoid focusing on your past because it is distracting and irrelevant to change. It might lead you to feed into a present narrative that is irrational, unproductive, chaotic, and stagnate.


Keep it Moving:


Walk forward and do not look back. Your destiny is in front of you, not behind you. By stepping forward, you have an unencumbered vision of your path. You will see potential trip hazards on the pathway to avoid getting discouraged. Do not walk backward in life. The backward direction is a distraction from your understanding that you have a mission ahead that needs your full attention.

# CHAPTER ELEVEN

# MAKE YOURSELF A PROFIT CENTER OF SURVIVAL ON EARTH

Making yourself a profit center on earth has nothing to do with accumulating monetary wealth. However, as a profit center, you are responsible for your existence on earth. When you are self-sufficient, you are free. When you are free, you are not beholden or entangled in the destructive standards of those who use money, power, fear, or manipulation to control your destiny.

You are responsible for your progress. Therefore, orient yourself to self-sufficiency. No one should have control over your spirit, soul, thoughts, and feelings. Do not create a codependent existence. Instead, you should seek support in your life from uplifting sources. It means that you should be self-sustaining.

Keep it Moving:

You should know your worth without compromise. Every human can survive and thrive based on their strengths and instincts. Therefore, you should work hard in your work environment. Apply your talents to the full measure of your ability. Maintain an internally high work ethic. Outpace, outwork, and maximize your invaluable presence in your career role. Your education or job matters less than the excellence and humility you embody. You will always be an invaluable profit center if you are highly responsible and have an unmatched work ethic.

# CHAPTER TWELVE

# DO NOT FOLLOW THE GOALS AND DREAMS OF SOMEONE ELSE

If you set your own goals and dreams, you will keep your objectives. When you find yourself in a directionless moment following behind someone else, remember that your independence is not being nurtured or actualized. Then, you will not engage in the codependent pursuits of others. Instead, tap into your internal power, and no one will ever be able to pull you from your passion.

Insecure people may recognize your gifts, use them, dispose of them, then try to devalue your worth. Hence, making you inextricably emotionally impaired in a codependent relationship. Whether it is a working relationship, friendship, partnership, family member, or organization, be mindful of your connections that do not match your internal survivability.

Keep it Moving:

The moment you feel that someone is making you feel insecure or dependent, move to the security of independence. If you set individual goals and routines, you will not drop everything to follow someone navigating you towards insecurities and codependency.

You cannot steer your own life when you are in the rear. So move to the front engine of your life and control your destiny.

# CHAPTER THIRTEEN

# LIFE IS A JOURNEY OF MANY QUESTIONS

In life, we have many questions but not all the answers. But you must keep moving if you believe more in yourself than the unanswered questions. If you continue with unrelenting faith, you will triumph if the road includes suffering; and prevail if the road contains failure. Our life journey is a complex path. The road buckles under us sometimes. But the road builds resiliency through the challenging times so you can come out on the other side to enjoy the wonders of life.

Keep it Moving:

If you keep moving forward on your life journey, you will have the flexibility of human existence with a victorious life. Celebrate every moment of love, joy, happiness, and peace to balance the rugged roads of difficulties and infirmities intertwined throughout your life. In the end, you will discover that you experienced more love, joy, happiness, and peace because you made it an unwavering goal.

# CHAPTER FOURTEEN

# DISTRACTIONS FROM YOUR POSITIVE NARRATIVES ARE DESTRUCTIVE TO PERSONAL DEVELOPMENT, GOAL COMPLETION, AND LONG-TERM MENTAL HEALTH

Each day allows you to change the life you have to the life you desire. It is critically important that you understand that externalized motivating factors are fleeting and not sustainable through the twists and turns of accomplishing goals. Internal motivations create sustainable support for dreams.

The indicators below demonstrate how external demotivating factors can distract you from your goals:

- You are constantly procrastinating
- Reflecting on other people's accomplishments
- Creating multiple excuses and repeating them in your head
- Participating in distracting, destructive, or time-wasting activities
- Setting up an infrastructure that will justify why you cannot begin your goals
- Adopting the marginalized categories that society has placed on you

Keep it Moving:

You must transcend external distractions that undermine your goals. Let your life story be a blazed pathway to fulfilling your dreams. But first, you must believe in your internal narrative to accomplish your aspirations. Avoid distractions of negative narratives at all costs.

# CHAPTER FIFTEEN

# IF YOU BELIEVE YOU ARE A PROCRASTINATOR, IT HAS MORE TO DO WITH YOUR BELIEF SYSTEM ABOUT YOURSELF THAN THE ACTS OF PROCRASTINATION

Negative belief systems are due to negative interactions or marginalized comments about your abilities in your past. As a result, you might believe that your deficits outweigh your attributes when accomplishing tasks. Procrastination could represent disorganized thoughts that do not allow you to begin or sustain tasks logically. Procrastination is the body's response to something worthy of accomplishment, and it is a process that takes time to execute.

Keep it Moving:

The next time you begin to procrastinate about a goal, remember it is something that your soul's DNA must fulfill. But the mind is telling you that you cannot accomplish the goal. That is why you create so much space in the unconscious brain stressing over not getting started.

Begin with the first step and make incremental steps towards your goal. Try not to anticipate reaching your goal's end but work on completing each micro-step. Completion of each step is a success toward your goal. Procrastination is a reversible belief system. So, take some action and neutralize the stagnation of procrastination to get started.

SEEK POSITIVE
ENERGY

# WE DECIDE TO WALK THROUGH POSITIVE OR NEGATIVE PORTALS OF ACTIONS, BEHAVIORS, THOUGHTS, AND EMOTIONS

Negativity does not provide hope because it does not possess light for a pathway. It is up to us to decide on a path of positivity or negativity. Negativity is a path of stagnation.

Growth means initiating boundaries to avoid negative interactions. Try to be mindful of which path pulls you towards your goals and which choices pull you away from your goals. The positive options navigate you toward your goals, and the negative choices pull you away from your goals.

Keep it Moving:

Do you notice that when you respond negatively or follow an adverse pathway, there is a negative counter-response that lingers? So, trust and follow the path of enlightenment with positive energy.

Do not compromise and follow harmful pursuits of people, places, or things that take you away from your goals. Destructive goals include unhealthy habits, procrastination, and pursuing things that prevent you from the light that supports your hopes and dreams. Instead, remain mindful of the positive energy that gets you closer to hope and dreams. Make this an unwavering goal.

You might feel alone, unfulfilled, or invalidated while others take the compromised road of negativity. Adverse and neutral sources of energy will create disorganized and distorted views ahead. The pathway with intense positive energy will make your way smoother for a comfortable journey. The smooth path happens when we are seeking positive outcomes. Although the roads are imperfect along life's journey, the pathway of positive light is developmentally healing.

*CHAPTER SEVENTEEN*

# NEGATIVE ENERGY IS ALWAYS CHASING EVERYONE EVERYWHERE, EVERY DAY

Unfortunately, too many people stop and entertain harmful and destructive pauses in their day instead of seeking positive energy to guide them. Always keep sight of who is in control. The world's negative energy tries to steal your joy, but God is right there, granting you mercy and grace to regain positive energy.

Keep it Moving:

Always start your day knowing you will have positive experiences and uncomfortable battles to navigate. Remember that the struggle between good and evil is daily. Do not lose sight of God's presence when you feel overwhelmed with negative energy emanating from all sources. Instead, call on positive resources that God has to offer. Refrain from getting confused by what you see in the world. Remember that God is the world and beyond. He is always in control. Do not get distracted but remember that God created everything in the world. Therefore, negative energy cannot reach the resources to help you fight daily battles.

# CHAPTER EIGHTEEN

# DO NOT ACT ON NEGATIVE THOUGHTS OR DEEDS TOWARD OTHERS

You cannot detach from your negative actions because they connect to your present and future outcomes. Adverse outcomes do not produce productive energy.

The energy created is energy gained. If you do not want negative energy, do not create it for others. You will retain negative energy to the measure you make in the universe. Atone for mistakes by asking for forgiveness from the Creator and those you have offended. Change your patterns that mimic past behaviors of negative energy.

Keep it Moving:

Rectify the wrongs of the past and release your life of bad energy. Exercising harmful deeds creates blocked energy that stifles relationships and positive trajectories of life goals. Filter your actions through positive energy and avoid negative energy unless you are comfortable living in the vortex of stagnation. Quickly ask yourself why you need to initiate a negative response instead of a positive method to move forward with a positive spirit. A positive reaction creates a longitudinal pathway to long-term positive gain instead of negative trapped energy. The more positively you interact with people, the more likely they will interact positively.

# CHAPTER NINETEEN

# WHILE ON THE JOURNEY OF LIFE, SIT IN JOY

Sit quietly and find out what joy means to you. Remember the steps you took to get to a place of joy and listen to your internal voice.

Keep it Moving:

Joy gives us the feeling of comfort and satisfaction to know that we can be happy. Therefore, when you achieve enlightenment, you should not turn your back but sit in the folds of happiness and appreciate the feeling.

People do not sit in their joy long enough to let it resonate through their bloodstream for longitudinal peace. Remember the importance of the quiet joy you feel in your soul. Create a balance of activities to strive for a joyous life.

# CHAPTER TWENTY

# SOME PEOPLE EXERCISE HARMFUL PARASITIC ACTIVITIES TO SELFISHLY ACCESS THEIR NEEDS BY TAKING ADVANTAGE OF PEOPLE'S TALENTS, REPUTATIONS, AND OVERALL GOOD ENERGY

People will attach themselves to you by complementing, gratifying, and glorifying you into submission to their agenda. This parasitic personality will offer monetary gain, camaraderie, career advancement, or friendship while taking advantage of your good nature. Be mindful of negative people attached to your positive energy, gifts, and talents to elevate their needs.

Keep it Moving:

Be aware of people's wit, charm, and engaging conversation. Watch and guard your mind, body, and spirit against parasites. When people drain your energy, their parasitic personality generally uses you for personal gain. Be aware of how you truly feel with people who are gaining more from your presence while you feel drained, confused, and disappointed. Realize that you are born with everything you need. You do not need the energy offered to you by everybody. If you must continue to be in the presence of parasitic people, remember your worth and protect the integrity and authorship of the spiritual energy you give away. Maintain positive energy and self-respect by maintaining a boundary for your mind, body, and spirit.

# CHAPTER TWENTY-ONE

# IT IS GOOD TO BE DECENT, KIND, HUMBLE, AND UNSELFISH WHEN THERE IS NOTHING TO GAIN AND NO ONE IS WATCHING

Do not feel embarrassed to have positive, ethereal, youthful qualities of unsoiled hope. Acts of goodness help you to transcend your stress when it arrives.

Keep it Moving:

Always seek good, decent, kind, humble, and unselfish narratives. When you feel good about yourself, you will recognize good people, jobs, and opportunities that uplift your life. You will have a compromised life filled with marginalization if you seek out compromised people, employment, or endeavors. Be decent, kind, humble, and unselfish. Your life will multiply with goodness, success, and loving human beings.

# CHAPTER TWENTY-TWO

# IF YOU ARE IN AN ENVIRONMENT WHERE YOUR TALENT THRIVES, DO NOT ASSUME THAT YOUR EMOTIONAL ENERGY IS ALSO THRIVING.

If your abilities match the environment, but your natural character calibration does not match the environment, ask yourself the following questions.

- Are your skills being utilized with integrity to your original purpose?
- Are your talents being packaged as someone else's without your permission?
- Do the people around you appreciate your abilities without respecting you?

Positive vibes are essential for the inventive mind. The creative spirit thrives in hearing the inner voice of the soul. When a creative mind does not have the freedom of inner peace, affirmation, positive vibes, and a platform of creativity, their creativity starts to diminish, then fade. A creative spirit must maintain creative environments. When creative minds do not create, it damages their mental health and mood balance.

Keep it Moving:

Even if you are in a place where you are working and tasked with giving your creative talents to your organization, make sure that you are creating in a positive mental space. You must still have control and freedom in your creative mind space to imagine unencumbered by external influences. Creatives are natural entrepreneurs because of the uniqueness of their creations. Their individualized desire to develop the manifestation of the images in their soul is intrinsically important. Therefore, remain true to your creative spirit and understand that creativity is not born in a hostile environment.

# CHAPTER TWENTY-THREE

# DO NOT FOCUS ON JUDGMENTAL PEOPLE

If judgmental people have critical space in their brains to analyze others, that is their problem. Why waste your time with their preoccupation? How much judgmental real estate space will you allow in your brain and soul? Are you spending time trying to force bad relationships, bad jobs, destructive behaviors, and harmful narratives about you or other people? Instead, remember to use your brain to focus on your own goals, improvements, and internal happiness.

Keep it Moving:

Refrain from harming your mental health by figuring out why people are judgmental. Judgmental people bring forward information to stagnate you, and insightful people will bring forward positive energy to enlighten you. The source of your negative thoughts can become more important than you as a productive person.

You produce your environment through relationships, jobs, behaviors, and internal narratives. Choose positive relationships, careers, behaviors, and internal dialogue, and you will maximize your real estate of positive energy in your life. Focus on your thoughts and emotions to promote positive cognitions, energy, pathways, and positive living. The only opinion that matters is your own.

# DEVELOPMENT OF THE PERSONALITY

# CHAPTER TWENTY-FOUR

# MANY PEOPLE FEAR BEING GREAT

You will follow other people's paths if you fear your own. Therefore, you must eliminate fear to avoid getting stuck on safe roads with no direction on other people's pathways. Greatness is a solo walk down an uncharted path.

Keep it Moving:

Fear locks you in comfortable nonchallenging directions. Traveling the highway of the masses can lead to resentment, sadness, loneliness, discontent, and a longing for congruency.

When you were a child, you had the innocence of clarity, vision, and the ability to block out negativity, restrictions, and limitations. Your path is set before birth by God without barriers. Do not allow the world to fill you with constraints. Be brave, cast fear away, and step forward. God is waiting for you on the journey. He is there with tools for you to succeed. He is the carpenter with a tool belt to make all things happen. Fear is not in God's tool belt.

Follow your path of goals and dreams. Include activities that help you to reach your full potential in life. Your faith, energy, hope, and inner courage will sustain you on the path.

# CHAPTER TWENTY-FIVE

# WHEN YOU ARE TALKING TO SOMEONE AND WANT THEM TO LISTEN, YOU MUST BE FORMULAIC ABOUT STARTING A DISCUSSION

Discretion, discernment, and timing are essential when knowing when to talk to someone for an effective outcome. Unfortunately, people often create a conversation about something important but do not consider a communication process of success.

Keep it Moving:

When you want to convey something significant, you can set the stage for good communication. Good communication includes discretion, discernment, and timing.

Utilization of discretion aims to figure out what communication works best for the person so they can hear you with accurate understanding. When you consider discretion in conversation, you are considering the discreet style of language that the person understands. If the person understands passive, straightforward, or universal language, utilize the style that conveys the information best to the receiver. Additionally, the speed at which you speak is also critical. Your speech should match the cadence and speed of the listener. Know what you will say and how you will say it so the message is understood. Otherwise, they will not feel fully invested in the shared information.

Communicating with discernment to others includes subjects of interest. Augment the information so the person will hear from a perspective that resonates with their ability to listen with understanding. Modify the content if you are conveying potentially diversionary, forward, or upsetting information to the receiver.

If the conveyors do not use discernment, they can shut down conversations. Use discernment by asking if the person is comfortable with the topic. It is crucial to bring up topics with a measure of bracketing.

Timing represents the optimum time to begin a conversation for the most effective outcome. When considering timing, you must consider the location, the number of people around, and the time of day, so the person is receptive. The location for the conversation is essential because the person has to feel comfortable in the space to receive the information and speak confidently about the information. If the person feels a lack of empathy, confidentiality, or comfort about the timing of the conversation, they will not be receptive to listening to the content.

It is also important to determine the number of people around when the conversation occurs. Most people prefer to avoid discussing difficult conversations in front of other people. Or a more extensive audience might create an optimum effect for the receiver to be more accountable and receptive to the conversation. All three components of discretion, discernment, and timing must be present to maximize effective communication.

# CHAPTER TWENTY-SIX

# WHEN YOU SAY THAT YOU CARE, IT IS NOT AN AUTOMATIC ACT OF CARING

Caring about a person must be put in motion unconditionally. You must care about a person during good times and bad. Can you care about a person when they are not making you happy? Do you put caring on hold because the person makes you upset? Caring is an unconditional character trait.

Keep it Moving:

If we are caring, the act of caring is a constant act, not a situational one. Therefore, continue developing actions representing a caring attitude for the people you love.

# CHAPTER TWENTY-SEVEN

# ACKNOWLEDGE NEGATIVE THOUGHTS AND ANGER

Generally, when you are angry, you are sad first. You are feeling dismissed, disengaged, and detached. What other people say or do can spark feelings of anger. Your anger represents your vulnerability that is difficult to contain.

If you cannot transcend anger, you need to consider why the other person triggers you to anger. What does the triggering event represent from your past? Finally, identify why the trigger impacted you so strongly.

Keep it Moving:

No one can make you act on angry feelings. People can do insensitive, mean, hurtful, dismissive, and cruel things, but how you respond demonstrates the security of your personality. Your self-esteem is built or torn down by your experiences as you develop. When people are insensitive, hurtful, dismissive, and cruel, it does not penetrate your soul if you have a strong sense of identity.

If you have a strong sense of identity, you will maintain control over your actions and how you respond to angry feelings. If you are angry, spend time determining the root of your anger and managing it from a healthier lens. Only you can make yourself mad, and only you can control madness in your life. Our internal soul and perception of the self are more important than the actions of others. Understand your anger so you can minimize it.

# CHAPTER TWENTY-EIGHT

# AUTONOMY DOES NOT MEAN SELFISHNESS, SELF-ABSORPTION, OR SELF-IMPORTANCE

Autonomy is an expression of uniqueness and outlier characteristics. It also should provide a deeper understanding of the individual emotional, cognitive, and physical space that others occupy and deserve to maintain.

Keep it Moving:

Your self-purpose and worth are encapsulated and untouchable for you, just as it is for others. Remember your self-worth without diminishing others. Understand that your uniqueness and outlier characteristics represent personal power. Refrain from eclipsing your development or others' ability to individuate.

# CHAPTER TWENTY-NINE

# IT IS ESSENTIAL TO RECOGNIZE WHEN YOU ARE WORRYING NONSTOP

You might be worrying so much that worrying is the first thing you think about when you get up in the morning and go to bed at night. You will look for the next thing to worry about because worrying is familiar to your daily routine. When you constantly worry about a problem, you are not solving it or putting your worries in their place.

Keep it Moving:

Resolving anxiety-provoking problems makes you better equipped to put your worries in perspective. Natural anxiety is in place to let us know that something within our control is out of order. Stress indicates that a problem needs to be solved or minimized.

Anxiety and worry are not there for you to take in as the problem itself. If anxiety feels like the main problem, it is because you cannot move anxiety and worry to solutions. Instead, anxiety and worry will become an overarching problem.

Do not focus on anxiety or worry in isolation. Alternatively, focus on the source of the concern. As soon as you start to worry or get anxious, let it trigger you to figure out the basis of your anxiety. Then consider a solution to your stress so you can minimize it.

The worst-case scenario source of your anxiety generally will not happen. So, take a deep breath and relax because your worst-case scenario is unlikely, so focus on solutions. Do not let worry and anxiety stagnate your happiness. Remember that anxiety is not more formidable than your capacity to access tools to get to the root of your anxiety and resolve it. Resolve anxiety as quickly as it arrives.

Take your time when you feel anxious. If you ignore anxiety instead of acknowledging it, it can become a tree of worry. You hold the seed of anxiety. Try not to plant the seed. Instead, look for solutions or instructions in the universe to eliminate your anxiety.

# CHAPTER THIRTY

# WHEN YOU KNOW YOUR WORTH, THE ROAD WILL OPEN FOR YOU

Even if you are still determining what to do next, you will succeed on the road destined for you when you know your worth. Self-worth sharpens throughout life if you are willing to sacrifice in humble environments, preparing you for a life worthy of your value. Self-worth does not allow you to succumb to buckling on the road.

Keep it Moving:

The route of opportunity makes you stronger. When you take on challenges beneath and above your reach, you will understand your worth. Do not be afraid to struggle but remember that it is preparation for the journey of a more substantial actualized existence that will make you proud.

# CHAPTER THIRTY-ONE

# MANY PEOPLE EXHIBIT MORALITY AND HOLD UP THE MANTLE OF RIGHTEOUSNESS FOR OTHERS TO FOLLOW

People will support upholding morality in spaces of justice, fairness, and equality. However, they lack the courage to actualize morality through courageous acts in support of others without gaining accolades.

Keep it Moving:

Be careful about who you follow as a moral compass, and make sure that you are not the one pushing morality without courage. Without a compass of morality, you will not be congruent to your righteous words. The actions of morality without courage are baseless character projections. Instead, be a person of integrity and make sure your righteousness matches your courage to act.

# CHAPTER THIRTY-TWO

# YOU CAN DO INTERNAL WORK ON YOURSELF TO DEAL WITH THE EXTERNAL WORLD

The objective is not to change your organic self to be more palatable to the world but to empower yourself to be resilient in the world. Sturdiness can come out of pain or challenging work. In this era of social media of likes, affirmations, followers, trolls, and ghosting enthusiasts, it is easy to lose sight of who you are. Caring about what others think about you gives them too much power over your development. Continue to develop the best version of yourself, not the standard set by others.

Keep it Moving:

If you follow your internal voice, you will be satisfied with your accomplishments, mindful of taking charge of your destiny, and not full of regret. Follow your inner voice of who you are and the visions of yourself in the future.

# CHAPTER THIRTY-THREE

# MANY PEOPLE LIVE A SYMBOLIC LIFE THAT MAKES SENSE ONLY TO THEM FROM THEIR SELFISH LENS

People who live a symbolic ego-driven life will give you a distorted reality to fit a crooked narrative filled with distortions.

Leading with a grandiose ego is a dangerous place to be, which includes an echo chamber of internal thoughts and close allies who endorse the narrative. The allies are like flies on the back of a horse who eat parasites that bother the horse. They are tiny wingmen with oversized egos who are not fulfilled.

The allies' objectives are to neutralize others around the grandiose personality and eventually neutralize the grandiose personality also. People in a mutually beneficial negative relationship create a vortex of neutralizing polarizing energy that ultimately neutralizes them.

Keep it Moving:

Be aware of the surrounding cast of influential people who support a parasitic narrative. They are ultimately parasitic on the leader they protect and the other people around them. So, these environments have no place for peace, productivity, or positivity. Instead, find environments that encourage open narratives that promote what is best for everyone.

# CHAPTER THIRTY-FOUR

# DO YOU FEEL INVISIBLE IN THE WORLD, LIKE WALKING AROUND AN ALTERED EXISTENCE BECAUSE YOUR CORE PERSONALITY IS KIND AND GENTLE?

Do you feel your kindness is a weakness? Kindness is a strength. It is easy to see how being kind is difficult when you walk around giving peace, love, and mercy and people are unkind to you and others.

You have been kind since childhood and are still surprised when people are unkind. It is not your nature to respond to people negatively or aggressively, even though situations might elicit that response. You do not have to level up to their aggression or lack of kindness to match other people's energy. You are baffled at the world and why you are supposed to navigate the cruel actions of others by changing yourself to match their energy level.

Keep it Moving:

The gift of kindness emanating from your soul is a strength from God. Hold fast and stay calm. Never let the world beat you so much that you change your energy. God knows your heart, and you will be protected when navigating the unkind actions of others. You should be humble in your giving of kindness but not diminish your self-worth. Give your kindness freely. You should remain strong in knowing God gave you the sacred qualities of kindness.

Trust that although your mind, body, and spirit are responding to the unfriendly actions of others, they will not penetrate you on a deep level if you maintain the goodness in your heart. Positive energy generates positive energy, and negative energy generates negative energy. Therefore, always respect yourself, and do not diminish yourself to allow another person to dominate you.

Only God has dominion over you. Therefore, regardless of how people respond to you, you should maintain the essence of your good heart. Stand up in a manner that maintains the calibration of your good soul and kindness. However, in doing so, you must retain your value and worth.

Your objective is not to change the other person or yourself but to respond in a way that creates effective outcomes, maintains your dignity, and fuels you with confidence to be kind in the world.

# CHAPTER THIRTY-FIVE

# IT WOULD BE BEST IF YOU NEVER LET AGE DEFINE YOU

Being too old or young has nothing to do with a person's development. A generation has nothing to do with someone's ability to accomplish goals. We are supposed to develop cognitively, emotionally, and psychologically daily. Every day we are supposed to allow the wisdom of experiences to build us beyond the last year, day, hour, minute, and second. There is a calendar and clock to keep up with the change in time.

Keep it Moving:

People who accomplish multiple goals without age limitations are focused on one perspective about time. They are laser-focused on one view of time, which is a timeline to accomplish their goals. They are not focused on their age. Stop placing limitations on yourself due to the numerical age timeline. People who achieve goals should not recognize the age variable in the equation. Their ability to accomplish goals defies time and age.

# CHAPTER THIRTY-SIX

# WHAT DOES IT LOOK LIKE TO TRANSFIGURE YOURSELF?

Transfiguring yourself is not what you think. It is not the adornment or augmentations you make to your outside appearance. Instead, your internal transfiguration equals grace, mercy, and love of self and others.

Keep it Moving:

When you impart an understanding of grace, peace, and mercy to others, you free yourself and others to make the world a better place. You elevate yourself to God's plan, which streams above the consciousness and darts of all and forever connects you to God's energy. So, grab your blessings and know that you are a blessing to yourself and others.

# INSTEAD OF TRYING TO FOLLOW SOMEONE ELSE'S BLUEPRINT, IGNITE YOUR LIFE NARRATIVE

Your DNA is already set in motion when you are born. So, naturally, it only takes a little energy to follow your DNA. But it takes a lot of power when you do not follow your DNA.

Fulfilling your DNA's natural qualities, gifts, and talents seems too easy. Following the route of your destined DNA and soul script is robust and broader and gives appearances that are too good to be true or too hard to get to the finish line. Soul scripts are longitudinal, natural to the soul, and complete in their creation for your life. We have free will to walk in the direction of our soul script.

Keep it Moving:

Your DNA has no previous pattern to follow but your own. Live your best life by following your soul script of joy, peace, and a leveled-up life. Follow the God-given pathway of your DNA soul script if you want to experience a vibrant life.

# IT IS IMPORTANT TO NOTE THAT POPULAR PURSUITS ARE ALREADY KNOWN AND EXECUTED

When you think like an individual, your idea is unique, and you are a trailblazer. So, blaze your path and let your legacy be a fulfillment of your skills and talents.

Keep it Moving:

Spend your time perfecting your talents and skills. Then, apply those skills without reservation. Master your abilities so that you are invaluable and can make a significant contribution based on your talents.

# CHAPTER THIRTY-NINE

# A RECEPTIVE VESSEL OF HUMANITY WILL ALWAYS LISTEN TO YOUR NARRATIVE

Do not expect empathy from someone who engages in negative interactions with you. If someone does not care about your voice, cognition, or emotions, do not expect them to have empathy for you. On the other hand, when someone listens to you intently, they empathize with you regardless of your philosophy.

Keep it Moving:

Your voice, cognition, and emotions are valuable. Find the right empathic spirit to guide you to an empathic understanding of your human spirit. Good listeners embody listening without interruptions, judgments, bias, or solutions. They understand the power of feeling, seeing, hearing, valuing, and attaching to the human dignity of individuality. These relationships provide valued solutions and insight.

# CHAPTER FORTY

# AN EXECUTIVE IS NOT NECESSARILY SITTING IN THE EXECUTIVE CHAIR

An executive can be at the receptionist desk, mailroom, janitor closet, or parking garage. They know who they are but have yet to come into their authentic role. Do not take anyone for granted or thwart their dreams. Be aware that you might be talking to your next boss. Open yourself up to affirming the lives of all people, and when they rise to the top, they will be mindful of your positive support. Positive connections span horizontally, vertically, zigzag, circularly, and all perspectives you can consider.

Keep it Moving:

We are all equal in the sight of God. Therefore, do not put yourself above humankind. Respect people's possibilities. Refrain from judging the status of where people are currently. Our positions in life are constantly shifting.

# CHAPTER FORTY-ONE

# PARENTS ALREADY HAVE A STRONG SPIRITUAL BOND WITH THEIR CHILDREN, SO THEY DO NOT NEED TO MAKE A MIRROR VERSION OF THEMSELVES

Allow your children to breathe from your oxygen until they can fly independently.

When a parent rejects a child, it mortally crushes their soul regardless of age. A parent-child relationship is strong based on the attachment at birth, and any emotional or psychological break initiated by a parent causes serious mental harm in children. If a parent creates a separation because the child does not conform, this invalidates the child's sense of self, purpose, and will to live.

Keep it Moving:

Remember that you are raising adults, not children. When parents implement confined parenting, they make their children undeveloped, codependent, insecure, and visionless. If you constantly devalue a child because they are not meeting up to your morality code, you are not ultimately helping their development. Development means you will instruct your child on navigating the world and give them a bracket of support to lean back and not fall.

If a parent pulls the rug from under a child entirely, all they do is fall straight to the ground. Your children are on loan from God. Care for your children by guiding them with positive, supportive tools to navigate the world.

Remember, as a parent, you have the most oxygen to fuel your child with the capacity to live a thriving life. The same is valid for carbon dioxide-type behavior that can kill your child with adverse mental health narratives. As a parent, determine if you believe in the ability to help your children to move developmentally in a positive direction. Bestowing grace, peace, and mercy is essential when developing a child into an individuated adult.

# CHAPTER FORTY-TWO

# SOME PEOPLE THINK THAT WHEN THEY HAVE BEEN RECEIVED, ENDORSED, OR HIRED, THEY BECOME GREAT AT THAT MOMENT

No organization can make you great. The creation of your life is a testament to the greatness of God and your individualized ability to become great.

Keep it Moving:

All people being equal with different talents and gifts, do not need external endorsements.

Organizations do not encourage individuals to achieve greatness above the organization. You are great because you dare to activate your uniqueness. Love your uniqueness. True love of self or others to individuate is a unifying love that equals the collective consciousness of the oneness of God.

# CHAPTER FORTY-THREE

# SOME PEOPLE FEAR EXPRESSING THEIR EMOTIONS

Fear stops people from expressing their emotions. It's easier for people to embrace the fear of silence instead of expressing their feelings. They believe if they don't express their feelings, all will be well with their relationships. Not saying your feelings give control to other people to interpret and determine mutual outcomes.

Your fear of expressing feelings will become more important than taking responsibility for your feelings and acting upon them. This type of narrative allows fear to have dominion over your life.

Keep it Moving:

Fear is an act of giving up your feelings to external power. You cannot fix what is not expressed and known. And what you do not know, you can't mitigate.

You can only alleviate your fears if you admit your feelings. Acknowledge your feelings and act upon them by talking about them, working on them, and implementing a change to respect your feelings and the importance of not ignoring them. This change will make you feel that your life is of equal importance and significance to others.

# CHAPTER FORTY-FOUR

# WHERE YOU ARE IS NOT WHERE YOU MUST BE OR STAY

When you are overwhelmed, your status feels like stagnating cement. You determine if you want to stay in a position of complacency when you already know there is a vision of something different that your DNA and birthright must actualize.

Keep it Moving:

Recognize when you are overwhelmed in your current state. Determine if your current life status is congruent with your internal comfort. Take a deep interior look and slowly change the trajectory of your current situation if it is not working for you. Your life is moving with every hour. Stop devaluing time and wasting away instead of igniting your life goals.

# CHAPTER FORTY-FIVE

# PEOPLE FORGET THAT THEY HAVE AN EXPIRATION DATE

People waste time being mad, afraid, vengeful, envious, jealous, and stagnant, waiting on someone else's gifts to rain down on them instead of fulfilling their destiny.

When you add up the time spent on resentful emotions, you will realize that you are moving further away from your goals.

Instead of executing harmful emotions, you should work on fearless goal setting; positive self-improvement; internal analysis of personal gifts and talents; and growth instead of goals of self-defeat.

Keep it Moving:

Learn to focus on bringing your talents and dreams into reality before your birthright expires. Stop wasting your time on stagnating behaviors of looking into people's life stories and coveting people's accomplishments, jobs, relationships, finances, and possessions. Stop wasting your time looking outward. Instead, work on your inward goal of creating a solid set of life objectives.

# CHAPTER FORTY-SIX

# YOU ALREADY KNOW THE ANSWER IF YOU ARE QUESTIONING, FEELING UNCOMFORTABLE, OR ASKING FOR ADVICE ABOUT AN AMBIGUOUS SITUATION

When a situation feels compromised, unsettled, or dangerous, it must be quickly assessed. The universe always speaks to us and tells us what to do immediately. Then our minds try to rationalize that our soul's instinct is incorrect. That would be wrong. Never ignore your instincts. Your internal soul wants to live, thrive, and seek positive energy.

Keep it Moving:

If your internal instinct tells you, something is not quite right, even by a small amount, stop, think, and process all the layers of the situation. If there are still blind spots and you cannot explain or rectify the feeling, do not move forward or proceed with slow cautionary steps.

Ideally, you will stop and get clarity on the blind spots of the scenario. Your soul is communicating to you that something feels unsettled or hostile. Your soul is the guidepost of a protective, positive life. If positive energy is your objective, do not ignore your soul.

# CHAPTER FORTY-SEVEN

# IF YOU LOVE HUMANITY, YOU WILL EXAMINE HOW OFTEN YOU SACRIFICE, STAND UP FOR, OR HELP YOUR FELLOW MAN

The more you offer to others, you will see yourself clearly. When you are vulnerable in your skin and give resources, talent, or time to another, it is a testament to true confidence in knowing that you have enough to offer. It will be replenished for unselfish giving. To walk through a valley of uncertainty by giving is to be a free spirit from attachments to things while acknowledging the power of the giving spirit that brings you peace, grace, and positive energy.

Keep it Moving:

The giver gets back what is more powerful than money or things. The giver receives freely from the universe deposits of positive energy that continue to grow and blossom and allow the giver to give more robustly. Trust in God and give generously with a love of self and others from a positive perspective. Embody your belief in God and keep moving. You have one chance to love when the opportunity comes. Don't let it pass you by.

# CHAPTER FORTY-EIGHT

# ARE YOU TRYING TO MAKE THINGS FRIENDLY AND PLEASANT WHEN THEY ARE NOT?

Are you trying to make something positive that feels negative? Are you in denial about negative friendships, jobs, organizations, and relatives that make you sad or anxious? It is okay if you are kind, empathic, and forgiving, but it does not mean you deserve maladaptive energy from people and environments.

Keep it Moving:

Acknowledging your truth is crucial for you to validate your feelings and thoughts. Try to be mindful of how you feel in unpleasant situations. Do a mental health inventory of who, what, where, and why the environment or people give off ambivalent energy.

Trust your emotional pilot light. If your emotions are triggered to sense negative energy, something in the environment is not congruent positively. Try to break down what is positive. Positivity makes you feel relaxed, supportive, and safe.

Neutral environments have conflicted energy that does not give you a straightforward assessment. In addition, these environments need to be more transparent, and the outcomes need to be clarified.

Negative environments are anxious, chaotic, stressful, and unstable. If your overall instincts inform you through anxiety that something is wrong, something is out of balance. Therefore, you must be mindful of your feelings and avoid the environment.

But it would be best to protect your mental wellness by internal empathic listening that lets you know when to back away from toxic environments.

# CHAPTER FORTY-NINE

# A BULLY HAS AN OBJECTIVE TO DIMINISH THE PERSON'S SENSE OF SELF

People are born with a sense of joy and happiness. When we are born, we seek a goal of enjoyment. We are not thinking about who we are in juxtaposition to everyone else. Our objective is to be happy and enjoy the little things in life. But a bully's objective is to get us to focus externally. When we are younger, we are internally focused on love, peace, and happiness placed there by God.

Keep it Moving:

Everyone in life is supposed to individuate. The bully wants us to externally focus on their version of who we are or who we should be. As we develop, we should individuate and fulfill our true calling and destiny of joy. If we focus on fulfilling the objectives of the bully, we cannot individuate and receive happiness. We are all outliers and have a calling in our life. We should never let anyone dictate who we are.

# ANXIETY IS A KNOCK ON THE DOOR THAT SOMETHING IS BOTHERING US

If we do not manage our anxiety and let it sit for too long, it becomes an overarching fear. Before you know it, we do not have control over the anxiety. Fear combines with anxiety and creates an overriding negative energy experience.

Keep it Moving:

Acknowledge that anxiety is present. The presence of anxiety is just the trigger to do something different because the current condition makes you uncomfortable and nervous. Anxiety is an indicator that you must remedy something in your life to move forward with positive rather than suppressed negative energy.

CHAPTER FIFTY-ONE

# ARE YOU SENSITIVE?

Do people say you are too sensitive, often cry, spend too much time remembering hurts, and have difficulty overcoming your emotions? Sensitivity means you have a deeper connection to the depths of your spirit. Do not feel guilty for the emotional connectivity that makes you empathic towards yourself and others.

It is better to be sensitive and care about the meaning behind emotions because they demonstrate a deeper form of communication that is organic and unfiltered.

Cognitive communication can be contrived or manipulated into inauthentic narratives. However, emotions are generally the clearest, natural form of communication. Not acknowledging your feelings or the emotions of others negates a true expression of communication grounded in people's souls. It is unrealistic to expect someone who doesn't understand feelings to understand yours.

It is healthier to be sensitive rather than insensitive. Tears and expressions of emotions are a healthy output of stressors on the soul. Generally, when people say you are too sensitive, they are uncomfortable with emotions. They have turned off this natural communication somewhere in their developmental history.

People who were told to turn off feelings, stop crying, or get over it, eventually stop expressing emotions. Or they experienced trauma or stressors that were not acknowledged, and emotions were not validated to the depths of their experience. Instead of understanding that their feelings should be validated, they learned to cope cognitively rather than express emotional pain or suffering. They devalue empathy for themselves and others. As a result, any outpouring of emotions from others triggers them, and they want your output of emotions to stop.

If people took the time to connect to someone's feelings, it would improve their attachment to each other. Unfortunately, not understanding someone's feelings creates an emotional detachment in the relationship. So, you are left feeling that your emotions are invalid, unwarranted, and not appropriate coping skills.


Keep it Moving:

It is better to be sensitive than insensitive. Sensitivity means that you have extra connectivity to the depths of your feelings and the feelings of others. Your connection to feelings gives you a deeper depth of empathy and neurological insight into the feelings you experience resulting from interactions with others. Your ability to acknowledge the inner workings of your soul has not been damaged by bracketing with cognitive rationale. The cognitive reasoning given by others as a way for them to explain away your emotions has to do with their history of emotions, not the validity of your feelings.

Your emotions are always valid and a healthy expression of your inner soul. Do not wait for someone to validate your emotions but assess why you have an output of emotions, what the triggers were, and how you can care for yourself in the future. Never invalidate your emotions due to someone else's low IQ of emotion processing.

# CHAPTER FIFTY-TWO

# WHEN YOU VALUE A HOUSE, CHAIR, OR SOFA MORE THAN THOSE WHO SIT ON THE FURNITURE OR LIVE IN THE HOUSE, YOUR CHAIRS AND HOUSE WILL EVENTUALLY BE EMPTY

Relatives, children, and friends will exit your home if they feel that the furniture and the building mean more to you than them.

Keep it Moving:

It is understandable if you value your house and its contents because you worked hard to obtain them. But you should not appreciate them more than those who visit or live in your house. When you make people secondary, you will soon realize that your companions are your home, furniture, television, cell phone, and computer.

Try to understand before it is too late that your relationship with people is irreplaceable and more valuable than things. Your furniture or house is not going to abandon you and get their feelings hurt if you talk to them poorly. But if you spill words of devaluation on people, they will not be around. If you choose people over things, you will select companionship over possessions; and have a more fulfilled life.

# GOD'S REACH

# CHAPTER FIFTY-THREE

# GOD SAID TO TRUST AND MEET HIM AT THE HIGHEST POINT

When you sit where there is no rooftop, you soar to connectivity to God without the world's barriers. Your seat of serenity with God has no confinement. Be at peace with the solitude of your destiny and your talent that connects you with God.

Keep it Moving:

Do not live life with regrets. Instead, push your possibilities forward and open your destiny. Remember to believe in your relationship with God to reach a higher level of truth and authenticity.

# CHAPTER FIFTY-FOUR

# WE ALL HAVE A ROAD TO DAMASCUS MOMENT WHERE WE ARE HUMBLED

On the road to Damascus, our previous reality of who and what we are immediately changed, and we need to recalibrate. This moment can be a moment of enormous grief, pain, illness, suffering, or loss. The depth to which the moment has occurred is the equivalent of a category five earthquake to the core of our identity, security, or health that can lead to a life-destroying or restoring episode.

Keep it Moving:

Look to the depths of the catastrophic episodic event and ask yourself how God is trying to move you forward swiftly without looking back. There is no room to look back, walk back, or start over backward.

Instead, find out the event's meaning quickly and move swiftly with goals that fit into your new reality. Trust that God is with you during the most profoundly complex challenges and happiest days. God's energy has not left you alone on your road to Damascus. His energy is manifesting at a higher level waiting for you to call on God, pray, and perceive a way forward. Work hard to achieve a way ahead, and remember that God is on all roads.

# CHAPTER FIFTY-FIVE

# GET ON THE ZIP LINE WITH GOD AND HOLD ON

Maintain your grip with the hands of God. Fly over jealous people, fraudulent offers, pride, external praise, negative feelings, sadness, insecurities, inflated ego, comparisons to others, feeling unlovable, unworthy, and incapable.

Keep it Moving:

Secure your hands to the Almighty, who loves everything about you unconditionally and holds onto you through every storm. If you are weak, God is lying down with you; if you are unsure, He is holding you steady; if you are hopeless, He is shining the path of possibilities. No matter what state you are in, God is there.

But remember, when you are ready to get busy with life to transcend your mental, physical, and psychological ailments, God will lift your hands and pull you as if you were on a zip line above all things. So remember to hold on until you are on the other side of victory.

# CHAPTER FIFTY-SIX

# SOMETIMES, PEOPLE TRY TO STEAL YOUR PEACE, GRACE, AND MERCY

Some people feel comfortable ripping at your spirit to see if they can break you. It is a sport to some to push people to unbearable stress. Instead, acknowledge who they are and process the depths to which they impact your well-being. Then, augment the relationship to a point where you can have balance.

Keep it Moving:

Your relationship with God might become tested when people try to make you feel that you are not worthy of who you are and what you have been given. But it is up to you to have an unbreakable connection with God. Avoid people who relish your sadness. Instead, put your faith in your unbreakable relationship with God. You are everything valued because He who created you is all things valued.

# CHAPTER FIFTY-SEVEN

# A PERFECT STORM IS WHEN GOD WANTS YOU TO WADE IN THE WATER TO TRUST AND WALK THROUGH THE MURKY WATER TO GET A BLESSING

A storm with murky water is perfect because it is one where your faith must transcend your fear and understanding of the weather and your abilities. You will not know the outcome of every gust of wind that blows you down, water that washes you away, or mud on your shoes, but it stops you in your tracks to think about what you know. You do know that in storms, it is between you and the force of nature that you cannot control. There is no control, but you are standing in an opportunity to exercise faith.

Keep it Moving:

God sees everything and wants you to be brave. In life, we have many storms. Refrain from leaning on your limited understanding and ability to manage natural life disasters from all sources. Since God controls the weather, it is best to trust God when you are in a storm.

# CHAPTER FIFTY-EIGHT

# DO NOT LET PEOPLE WEAPONIZE YOUR LOVE OF GOD AGAINST YOU

People might want to attach to your spirit, which exemplifies your belief in God. People might use your attachment to God to disarm or judge you and weaken your attachment. When people weaponize God against you, they will engage in many activities to attach to your spirit of positivity without appreciating the origin of your positivity. You must be aware of people's attachments to you that can compromise or test your faith.

People may hire you to cover up the negative energy in an organization, become your friend so you can project good vibes among their friends, or support your talents so they can control your development.

Your allegiance to God makes your heart open to people. Make sure that your attachment to God does not waiver with negative energy experiences with people. Hostile environments and people can drain your love, peace, grace, mercy, and joy.

Keep it Moving:

Do not lose sight of your love of God, and continue to exude love, grace, peace, mercy, and joy. Love God with all your heart and soul, and do not let anyone overshadow your relationship with God. You should be aware of people seeking to attach to you for their gain. It is important to remember that when your faith is feeling compromised, you need to assess if someone is weaponizing your godly qualities for their advantage. Guard against distress inside of yourself. Learn to protect the God spirit in you.

If you are unsure of what is happening or what you are feeling with certain people, it is a red flag that something needs to be more transparent.

With God, everything is positive, clear, and transparent. But if you feel that someone is questioning your relationship with God or they are encouraging uncomfortable behaviors, it is a fundamental problem. So create a comfortable or permanent barrier until you know whether this relationship is compromising your relationship with God. Then proceed with the clarity of God.

# CHAPTER FIFTY-NINE

# DO YOU HAVE CONSTANT CONTACT WITH GOD

Many people have continuous contact with their social media, friends, jobs, perceived power, and material things. But they fail to remember the origin of all that they have emanating from God. People think that material things require constant contact and pursuit.

In life, we are subject matter experts on many things. Therefore, learn to be a subject matter expert of God. Learn to embody a Godly spirit. In this way, God will endorse and support your plans. Since God has placed a specific calling on your soul, your hard work and humbleness will find electricity in the planet for your goals.

Keep it Moving:

Nothing you have needs your constant contact more than your internal soul and the souls of the people who are important to you. God is the origin of everything. The things in the world distract and undermine your constant contact with God. When social media, convenience friendships, jobs, titles, power, money, and material things are at the forefront of your connection, remember that you are ignoring the source of everything.

Become in constant contact with God. He will guide you to situations and people where your life fulfillment is boundless beyond anything you can acquire on earth. Follow God always, and He will fuel your abundant life. When you get distracted with things in the world, remember the Holy energy inside yourself to surpass everything.

# CHAPTER SIXTY

# ON SOME DAYS, 1 + 1 EQUALS 0, AND EVERYTHING ADDS UP TO A NEGATIVE VALUE

God is on the throne, and the whole world is his church. Do not lose sight of God. Every day ask God to carve you out of your blind spots that are not productive. Faith removes blind spots. Blind spots make us blind to the growth and development of ourselves from past and current maladaptive behavior. Eliminating demotivating zero-sum behavior and thoughts makes room for productive behavior that leads to good outcomes.

Keep it Moving:

Stop holding on to the zero-sum blind spots in your life. Eliminate all toxins from your spiritual, emotional, physical, cognitive, and material life that are old habits that tear down your confidence. Instead, make space for the new you that embraces the infinite multiplier of God in your life.

# CHAPTER SIXTY-ONE

# HELL IS A MOUNTAIN OF JUDGMENT THAT YOU PROJECT AND RECEIVE

When you judge, it spills onto you like a disease. Judgment stifles like carbon dioxide to humans who accept it and bestow it on others. Judgment is a weakened perspective in the soul. It creates internal and external arrested personality development. Judgments of others show that we are frail in our self-confidence and lack the perspective to accept the personhood of others.

Keep it Moving:

Empathic understanding trumps judgment. A person's empathetic perspective bestowed on others is understanding other people's lived experiences. Perspective helps people to see the person from a nonjudgmental lens. An open view of analysis gives you an open mind to know the other person without bias. Hence, stop tripping over a mountain of negative energy of active judgment. Instead, try to self-reflect on why you have so much time to judge people instead of working on self-improvement.

Be mindful of your frustration that leads to an externalized analysis of others instead of creating a life of personal development. Unless you live a life of absolute developmental perfection and infinite nirvana, you do not have mental or emotional space to assess anyone else's developmental life but your own.

# CHAPTER SIXTY-TWO

# FORGIVENESS IS FREEDOM FROM THE CHAINS OF WHAT SOMEONE ELSE HAS DONE TO YOU

If you keep thinking about past transgressions by brooding over them or acting like the offender still has power over you, the person who imparted the adverse action gets the space to change how you think about yourself developmentally. No one deserves to have this much power.

Think about the stagnating narrative of the transgression and how it limits you emotionally, cognitively, and physically. Live up to forgiveness and exaltation of God's goals for you with boundaries of protection from more harm in the future.

A lack of forgiveness represents rigidity that does not allow you to acknowledge feelings and experience closure of those feelings. If you forgive, you will be able to recognize your emotions and your security to know that you can move past anything negative.

Keep it Moving:

Free yourself from a lack of forgiveness and repeating a narrative inside your head about the wrongdoing imparted by others. Refrain from living down to their impression of you.

Forgiveness is an act that requires a higher level of intellectual understanding and spirituality. But, whether you are young or old, wealthy or impoverished, well-educated or modestly educated, it doesn't stop you from having the value of forgiveness.

You will live up to forgiveness and the exaltation of your mind, body, and spirit when you embrace the magnitude of forgiveness instead of the limitations of negative energy that someone else thought you deserved.

When you forgive others, you are looking forward to what you can make happen in the future. Therefore, the past mistakes of others have no relevance in your future.

People who have the capacity to forgive know their worth beyond distinctions of human qualities. They are self-confident and humble at the same time. Their mind constantly moves to harness positive energy so they can move forward in relationships and opportunities to live life without roadblocks.

# CHAPTER SIXTY-THREE

# SOMETIMES, WE BLAME GOD FOR OUR CHALLENGES AND SAY IT IS OUR CROSS TO BEAR

Challenges are bound to occur because of the continuity of engagement as an imperfect human among imperfect humans. But minimization of the detrimental impact of challenges is a possibility. Appropriate actions can neutralize stress and problems in life.

Ask God for coverage when the stress begins. Allow the Holy Spirit to enter your thoughts and prayers when your discernment tells you something is wrong. Sit in silence and listen to the word of God. Allow positive energy to penetrate your thoughts or actions that lead to solutions from God.

Keep it Moving:

When we sit in our challenges, we need to focus on God and ask for insight and a way through a complicated pathway. In the silence, we can hear the spirit of God guiding us toward His love of peace and mercy. When we think there is negative energy around us, remember that God is always above all negative energy. Look above when strife, confusion, struggle, and pain are all around you, and ask God to place you on higher ground with His love and security.

# CHAPTER SIXTY-FOUR

# THE POWER DIFFERENTIAL CONSTANTLY SHIFTS IN ORGANIZATIONS THAT PROMOTE A POWER BASE

A shifting power base does not allow you to grow in your personal development. Remember that God is the source of all energy.

You will strive, fumble, or coast depending on how you identify yourself within an organization. When participating in an organization, you will flourish if you bend to the organization, fumble if you are trying to make things fair, and coast if you stay under the radar without helping yourself or others in your organization.

Striving, fumbling, and coasting lead to a life of push and pull on your development. Leaning into an organization's power does not help to develop the personality. Instead, you grow only by understanding your power fueled by God.

Keep it Moving:

A personal calling is untouchable by organizations unless you intentionally compromise it. No organization or person can augment your power. God created your strength, and no one can touch it, take it away, or compromise it but you. God holds the real power. He has given it to you.

You give up your energy when you strive, fumble, or coast with compromised organizations. You can ignite your power or act like it doesn't know it exist. However, God created the pilot light, not any organization, and you can ignite your unstoppable personal power.

# CHAPTER SIXTY-FIVE

# AFTER YOU HAVE TRIED TO TALK TO SOMEONE TO SOLVE A PROBLEM WITHOUT SUCCESS, LOOK INTERNALLY

Go into a quiet place inside your soul and sit in silence. The quiet calm place is the essence of God. As you sit in silence, come up with solutions to every problem you ponder. You might hear a lot of mundane information come into your head, but eventually, the quiet data from God comes.

Listen to your soul where God dwells. God will give you information that is calming, less catastrophic, solution-oriented, and overall good energy. When God guides you, the problem feels lighter, positive, and hopeful, with an insight-filled road.

Keep it Moving:

Solutions dwell in the quiet peace of silence. Seek silence when you are stuck and have exhausted all solutions. The answer lies inside your soul, which is the dwelling place of God. Silence helps to understand the invisible narratives of ethereal insight and successful outcomes.

# CHAPTER SIXTY-SIX

# RECEIVING GOD IN YOUR LIFE MEANS ACCEPTING THE HUMBLE GIFTS THAT HE HAS PUT ON YOUR SOUL

Respect the positive character attributes that you possess. Kindness, empathy, reliability, responsibility, love, selflessness, friendship, charity, and forgiveness are the superpower gifts that drive your talents and goals to the stratosphere. When you follow your modest skills, you will receive the love of God. Embrace the internal love that He has affirmed in you, and the gifts He has bestowed on you will fuel a magnificently fulfilled life.

Keep it Moving:

Remove the noise of insecurities, personal judgments, perceived limitations, and hopelessness that blocks your future. Remember that God makes no mistakes and created you with perfection in your gifts. He has given you all the talents you need to manifest God's love, and the world cannot destroy it. God created people in His image, and He did not exclude you. So, embrace your gifts, and don't turn your back on what God has given you. Believe in God above all the universal barriers that do not help you to hear Him.

# THE WALK WITH THE CREATOR FEELS LONELY AT TIMES BECAUSE YOUR WALK WITH THE CREATOR IS UNIQUE AND UNMATCHED

You are not alone. God's angels are all around you in plain sight and manifested in the serendipitous acts of others. God allows us to have a bounty of destined creativity, activating a vibrant life of wonders and uniqueness. You are an outlier who is one of a kind, with a unique soul that must fulfill itself. Although it might feel like the people closest to you are not backing up your dreams, God brings in an army of guardian angels at your lowest points when you think you cannot move forward.

Whether sitting in a room filled with people or at a solo table in a restaurant trying to gather yourself, God is there waiting for you to put his mission in motion. So don't give up on yourself and your soul script. No one has a window to your soul but God and your guardian angels, so do not wait for others to step up or offer a hand up.

Keep it Moving:

Be mindful that a unique destiny is individualized. Even though your future might feel lonely, be careful about seeking a cheering squad.

Sometimes the cheering squad can be a healthy recharge, but sometimes the cheering squad can be a distraction. It is essential to know the difference. Lean into the Creator and seek the ultimate cheering squad that uplifts your creativity.

# CHAPTER SIXTY-EIGHT

# WHEN YOU FOLLOW THE PATHWAY OF GOD, YOUR PLANS ARE ALREADY FUELED

Follow God when you feel sad, distracted, or unmotivated.

Keep it Moving:

God's path is always precise and predictable. God's direction equals love and support. God's plan will not stop, so why should you give up on God's plan for you?

When the new day dawns, your plans are already set in motion. Even if you are disengaged and cannot figure out the plan for the day, use your feet and make the first step of the day fueled by faith.

# CHAPTER SIXTY-NINE

# THE WORLD IS A PLACE TO DISCOVER MORE OF GOD'S GOODNESS IN PEOPLE AND UNIQUE PLACES

Attach to the positive energy in God's people and environments when you are in an area that does not feel Holy. Then, ask the Holy Spirit to enter that space or relationship for coverage until you create a healthy barrier.

Keep it Moving:

In Godly environments, God's energy is all around. Building fortitude takes a lot of internal and external strength in adverse environments. Always acknowledge when you are in compromised negative energy and ask The Holy Ghost for backup.

# CHAPTER SEVENTY

# IF YOU ARE NO LONGER DREAMING AND INSPIRED, REMEMBER THAT FEAR AND HOPELESSNESS ARE PROBABLY PRESENT

When you stop dreaming and lose inspiration, you have forgotten your exceptionality and lost your belief that you can dream. When we are children, we do not understand boundaries but see the vision of who we can be in the future. Do not let this low point steal your joy and connection to life and God that moves you forward.

Keep it Moving:

Be patient, and do not be afraid. Remember, God is pure love, and there should be no fear or hopelessness in love. The perception of loneliness of not being connected to people or goals distorts the true purpose of life. You will connect to your inner God spirit by plugging into hope and dreams.

Some places have boundaries, but the simplicity of life without limits is where the spirit of God dwells. Hopes and dreams represent boundless possibilities. When you have landed on the right pathway, there are no barriers. You no longer experience hopelessness but an ongoing season of God. Let your embrace of the love of God be your goal for all things.

# CHAPTER SEVENTY-ONE

# IF WE LOVE OURSELVES OR OTHERS BLINDLY WITHOUT FIRST ATTACHING TO THE HUMBLE SPIRIT OF GOD, WE WILL NOT MAKE ROOM FOR GREATER LOVE

The Greater Spirit of God represents humility, the ability to develop change, and unconditional love of self and others. The connection of God's love of self is the highest level of love that a person can achieve. God's love allows us to attach to significant relationships regardless of flaws and limitations at a higher level.

Keep it Moving:

True love of self or others is a unifying love that respects people's spiritual souls, flaws, and ability to change. Your source of love and development is never more bountiful than the Holy Spirit. Therefore, embrace the Holy Spirit if you want a greater connection to the true power of love.

# RELATIONSHIPS

# CHAPTER SEVENTY-TWO

# THE NUMBER OF POSITIVE RELATIONSHIPS PROVIDES THE INGREDIENTS FOR A POSITIVE LIFE

The more positive relationships you have will determine how positive your life will be. Positive energy relationships create a sense of balance with your mind, body, and spirit. It gives you physical, emotional, and cognitive peace and serenity.

Relationships are more valuable than anything that you might possess. If you think deeply, relationships are the one thing that can bring you true joy, laughter, inspiration, encouragement, support, love, grace, and mercy. If you choose your relationships wisely, you will have positive connections, experiences, memories, mental health, physical health, and overall wellness to endure stress. Our daily interactions in relationships impact our mood, relaxation, and motivation to thrive in life.

Keep it Moving:

Your focus should be on obtaining and maintaining positive relationships with people who bring you positive energy. Connections supply us with husbands, wives, partners, friends, mentors, colleagues, and opportunities. An investment in relationships pays higher dividends in life than any stock on the stock exchange. Human capital with positive energy is the best investment in a life of wellness.

# CHAPTER SEVENTY-THREE

# DO YOU FEEL ISOLATED, ALTHOUGH SOCIAL MEDIA GIVES YOU ACCESS TO MILLIONS OF PEOPLE AND OPPORTUNITIES?

Are you trying to figure out why your hundreds of Megabyte friends and followers do not know you, although some are organic friends? Do they know when you have pain and suffering? Or do they represent a bit, nibble, byte, kilobyte, or megabyte friendship in cyberspace without feelings or empathy?

Consider the reality of your relationships and demand an investment of oxygen-to-oxygen organic face time with the people who matter to you. Are you trying to figure out why friends think a one-sentence text is okay? Do you feel the connectivity to friends who believe it is sufficient to text you? Friends who take the time to call or FaceTime you are the ones who understand your need for connectivity of shared love, kindness, and support.

Are you trying to figure out why an organic connection in dating is virtually nonexistent? It is hard to connect to people organically when your only resource is in the one-dimensional kilobyte world. Instead, spend time exploring people in natural environments of parties, concerts, sporting events, bookstores, coffee shops, dinner parties, brunch day parties, organization meetings, hikes, and time with friends. You will meet more people kinetically and authentically than online.

People will not mislead and ghost you in cyberspace if you meet in real-time to determine if you vibe organically. Then you can be accountable for your genuine empathic feelings.

Are you trying to figure out why your grandmother, grandfather, favorite aunt, or uncle does not remember your birthday? Did you remember to call and visit them face-to-face? All people fade away with a lack of connectivity. They lose the enjoyment of seeing, hearing, feeling, and touching. Human beings, by nature, are socially oriented, and one-dimensional existence is not how human beings can flourish.


Keep it Moving:

Without organic connections, there is no genuine connection. We are created in the flesh, not the kilobyte. You can connect to people authentically. Take time to cultivate synchronistic, real-time connections. Asynchronous relationships, although convenient, are not feasible for organic socialization. Video synchronistic encounters help; however, they do not engage all human senses.

Generations of disconnected people are online daily. They are searching for asynchronous connections instead of real-time connectivity where they can see, hear, smell, touch, and connect the kinetic energy between two humans.

Online we are packed with megabytes of people's data while in a desert of organic human connectivity. Get out of your one-dimensional existence in cyberspace. Develop organic meetings with your friends, family, colleagues, and organizations. Then you will experience tactile, seeing, hearing, feeling, and thinking human beings with humble agendas to connect organically with others. Organic relationships are the exhilarating human connections that make you feel that you are not alone on this journey of life.

# CHAPTER SEVENTY-FOUR

# EXISTING WITHOUT GOOD COMMUNICATION REPRESENTS EXISTENCE WITHOUT BEING SEEN OR HEARD AUTHENTICALLY

Productive communication is necessary for building healthy relationships and accomplishing goals. Living without good communication leads to developing lines of communication that can collide, crisscross, and coexist with blind chaos.

If you have included havoc, chaos, dismissive, selfishness, and one-sided communication in your relationship, this is not a bonded relationship. There is a difference between a relationship and tolerant obedience to another person. Tolerant obedience is not an authentic relationship of balanced mutual goals. Poor communication does not allow for relationships to develop in sync.

Keep it Moving:

Build healthy communication that can create a coexistence between two people trying to grow and develop together. Be mindful of considering the other person's whole perspective if you wish to walk parallel in mutual goals of good communication. Good communication has a foundation in the following steps when speaking with another person:

- Listen without interruption or trying to process what you will say next while the other person is speaking.
- Express how you understand the other person's perspective.
- Ask if you have interpreted their perspective accurately.
- Reflect in a way that the person can hear you positively.
- Express how you can put the other person's sentiments into action to improve communication.
- Build a relationship with the philosophy of being heard and listening.
- Listening starts with respect for your internal voice. Then you can create a mutual understanding that all perspectives are valued.

A relationship cannot sustain itself on its own. Mutually respectful communication and action maintain a relationship, not an unconscious belief system that good communication exists where it does not. Immediately, embrace your inner narrative to bond with others instead of a one-sided obedient relationship. Good communication is a dialogue, not a monologue of polarizing narratives.

Therefore, respecting both perspectives creates good communication. Just respecting the narrative of the dominant orator is not going to help a relationship to bond. If one partner is more swift with words, quick to speak up, or a wordsmith, it does not mean that their narrative is more valid or predominant. The common denominator is that the relationship has two people; if the relationship thrives as one unit, both voices need to be valid and predominant. Respecting the duality of narratives in a relationship is the only way for a relationship to thrive based on mutually beneficial communication. Finally, good communication builds a foundation for an authentic in-sync relationship of compassion, love, and respect.

# CHAPTER SEVENTY-FIVE

# WHAT IS YOUR RELATIONSHIP WITH MONEY?

Do you elevate money as your primary focus? Do you assume that acquiring money makes you happier; a better person; more physically desirable; problem free; in control; validated; socially acceptable; and immune to problems? All these assumptions are false. Money is a source to make purchases and pay for services.

Keep it Moving:

The possession of money in your life does not give your personality currency. But many people believe this to be the case. So do not default to gaining, coveting, or compromising your integrity to acquire money. People will spend a good portion of their life acquiring money.

They will acquire education at expensive prominent schools to maximize earnings later. Then they pursue careers that they detest for monetary gain. Additionally, they attach to high money-earning partners instead of love relationships. These actions can accumulate more money and stress that compound soulless endeavors, adding to more pressure if the money runs out.

Money does not create character enhancements, ethics, significant positive relationships, or an increased social IQ. Money cannot provide you with a better personality. Work hard to invest in the development of your personality organically without a monetary identity. Balancing the perspective of money and its proper place in your life will supply a wealth of peace.

# CHAPTER SEVENTY-SIX

# WHAT IS YOUR RELATIONSHIP WITH HUMAN FRAILTY?

As humans, we must embrace our birth and our final chapter. This common destiny that we share creates connectivity in the human experience. Although our experiences are different, our shared thread of space on earth should offer mutual mercy.

Keep it Moving:

Our relationship with ourselves and humanity will represent sin, mistakes, failure, disappointment, and chaos due to our free will of choices and fragility as humans.

Accept humility, forgiveness, mercy, grace, and love for imperfections in the human journey. If God loves you, why don't you love him back by accepting love for yourself and others? Understand that the love you receive from God is the love you should give generously with free will.

# CHAPTER SEVENTY-SEVEN

# LEADERS SERVE AT THE PLEASURE OF THOSE THEY LEAD

Followers bestow leaders with the freedom and right to teach them. Hence, leaders should maintain humility and dignity in their privilege to lead. Furthermore, leaders should value and understand their responsibility to be visionary and supportive of the people who enable their title of leader.

Keep it Moving:

However, if leaders do not value their followers, followers can use their feet and leave under their leadership.

# CHAPTER SEVENTY-EIGHT

# WHAT IS YOUR RELATIONSHIP WITH ANGER?

Do not get mad at other people's weaknesses. Your anger represents your vulnerability that you cannot transcend. If you cannot control your anger, you must consider why the other person triggers your anger. What does the triggering event represent from your past? Who in your past made you angry in the same way? Identify why the trigger impacted you so strongly.

Keep it Moving:

Take a deep breath and determine why you have given the other person so much control to bring you to a state of giving up your power. Use silence, and do not respond when you are angry. No good emanates from angry rants. Current nor future relationships prevail in angry discourse. Instead, spend more time determining the root of your anger and managing your discontent from a healthier lens. Only you can make yourself mad, and only you can control madness in your life.

# CHAPTER SEVENTY-NINE

# YOU MIGHT FIND YOURSELF IN A RELATIONSHIP WHERE YOU PULL THE MOST WEIGHT FINANCIALLY, SOCIALLY, OR PROFESSIONALLY

We often forget at the beginning of our relationship when we were choosing characteristics of the souls that we are negating the operations and management of the relationship.

These factors might be null of romantic variables, but they are factored into the successful management of the household regardless of the connection of the souls. However, the foundation of love and a soul connection is pliable tissue between two people that gets you to the discussion about fixing the cracked and broken pieces of the marriage. Conversely, brittle tissue relationships without love or soul connections can easily be vulnerable and do not reconcile differences.

Keep it Moving:

There is a logical reason you chose your partner, which probably has nothing to do with finance, socializing or a profession. Does the person bring intangible things like peace, love, unconditional support, and joy? Does that person make you feel calm, happy, and loved? Well, that is worth humbling yourself to climb off the tower of external pillars that do not make an emotional relationship thrive in private.

Assess what you truly need in a relationship and remove the analysis of external influences. Tap into the positive qualities of your mate, nurture, and build those qualities to benefit your marriage.

A bond of the connective tissue of love, mercy, forgiveness, and grace in a partnership allows you to discuss, recalibrate, and reposition factors in your life to maximize a positive, thriving relationship.

# CHAPTER EIGHTY

# YOUR SUCCESS OR FAILURE IS IMPACTED BY OTHER PEOPLE WHEN THEIR FEELINGS OR THOUGHTS AFFECT YOU

Your emotions and instincts are exclusively yours. Emotions emanate from your soul.

No one hears or feels them like you do. When you reveal the depths of your feelings to someone else, you subconsciously seek affirmation, support, or endorsement. The objective is to validate your feelings regardless of other people fully understanding your emotions.

Keep it Moving:

Make sure that when you share your emotions, you know that the person will give you unconditional validation, support, and inspiration for growth. But more importantly, you never need to justify your feelings, but you do need to validate your feelings.

# CHAPTER EIGHTY-ONE

# WHAT IS YOUR RELATIONSHIP WITH THE SUNRISE?

Do you look at the sunrise as a gift? Do you look at a new day as every day or an opportunity for life's goals and experiences?

When the new day dawns, do you get up, pray, meditate, shower, exercise, and set goals? The light of a new day is an opportunity to grow and develop. Do not sit and wait around for the day to unfold. Make it a purposeful day.

Keep it Moving:

Every day is a gift from God. When you get a gift, you will generally open it with wonderment, excitement, enthusiasm, and gratitude. So the dawn of a new day should commence with the youthfulness of boundless possibilities, regardless of how many days you have already experienced on earth.

Even if you know that you'll be doing the same thing, working the same job, or in the same status as yesterday, it is up to you to bring wonderment, excitement, enthusiasm, and gratitude.

As beings of free will, it is up to us to open each day as a gift and infuse an expectation that today will be more insightful, happier, and fulfilled. The new day is a unique opportunity for change, love, and experiences of gratitude. So, move forward and give your daily attention to the highest level each day!

Always keep it moving.….

Life will bring you suffering at times because this is a part of the human experience, and suffering does not pass anyone. But most important is that life will bring you happiness, laughter, joy, and hope again to the measure you believe in transcending your suffering.


Keep it Moving:

Remember that suffering is part of life, but it should not be your life story. When suffering comes, process, pray, and prepare to be mentally, psychically, and emotionally strong to transcend your suffering. Prepare for healing, not continued suffering. Visualize resilience to regain hope, joy, and healing.

Write down six goals that will allow you to individuate and realize your true talents, DNA, and calling. Anything you have visualized for yourself is already a reality written on your soul. It is up to you to decide that you will put steps in motion to bring your dreams into successfully manifested goals.

1.

2.

3.

4.

5.

6.